150

PARTY DRINKS

150

PARTY DRINKS

hamlyn

First published in Great Britain
in 2004 by Hamlyn,
a division of
Octopus Publishing Group Ltd
2–4 Heron Quays,
London E14 4JP

ISBN 0 600 61172 8

A CIP catalogue record for
this book is available from the
British Library

Printed and bound in China

10 9 8 7 6

Notes

The measure that has been used in the
recipes is based on a bar measure,
which is 25 ml (1 fl oz). If preferred, a
different volume can be used providing
the proportions are kept constant within
a drink and suitable adjustments are
made to spoon measurements, where
they occur.

Standard level spoon measurements
are used in all recipes.

1 tablespoon	=	one 15 ml spoon
1 teaspoon	=	one 5 ml spoon

Imperial and metric measurements
have been given in some of
the recipes. Use one set of
measurements only.

US	UK
granulated sugar	caster sugar
maraschino cherries	cocktail cherries
toothpick	cocktail stick
heavy cream	double cream
presweetened cocoa powder	drinking chocolate
confectioner's sugar	icing sugar
pitcher	jug
lemon peel or zest	lemon rind
light cream	single cream
club soda	soda water

SAFETY NOTE

The Department of Health advises that
eggs should not be consumed raw. This
book contains recipes made with raw
eggs. It is prudent for more vulnerable
people such as pregnant and nursing
mothers, invalids, the elderly, babies and
young children to avoid these recipes.

Contents

Introduction

Just as the types of social occasions under the banner of 'party' range from formal cocktail parties to informal al fresco gatherings, themed events or intimate dinner parties, the range of drinks that can be served at parties varies widely, too. Browse through the chapters in this book and be inspired by recipes for all occasions. Whether you want to serve an informal punch for guests to help themselves from a glass bowl, a long refreshing drink in tall glasses at a summer barbecue, a hot toddy for chilly winter nights or a pick-me-up for overnight guests the morning after the night before, you are bound to find something among these pages that will appeal to your taste buds.

You don't need much equipment nor to buy every party mixer available. You'll only end up with a cupboard full of obscure cocktail ingredients that will never be used!

Concentrate instead on supplying just one or two cocktails at your party, along with the usual selection of beer, wine and soft drinks and you won't go far wrong.

Ice and glassware

Ice is an essential at parties but bear in mind that it is required to keep drinks cool, not to dilute them. Drinks recipes may specify crushed ice or cracked ice. Crushed ice cools a drink more effectively and more quickly than cracked ice but too much of it will dilute a drink too fast. Use cracked or crushed ice rather than ice cubes for drinks that require blending, to save damaging the blender blades. Make your own cracked ice by filling a strong polythene bag or a clean tea towel with ice cubes and hitting them with a rolling pin; for crushed ice, simply smash the ice harder!

If you cannot make enough ice cubes yourself at home,

remember that many supermarkets, small stores and petrol stations now sell bags of ice cubes. Similarly, if you don't have enough glasses for guests at your party, you'll have to get some in. Plastic disposable ones are an option although people always prefer drinking out of proper glasses. It is possible to hire these from catering outlets or off-licences although many supermarkets will now loan you glasses at no cost at all. When serving hot drinks in glassware, first put a metal spoon into the glass and pour the hot liquid over the spoon to help prevent the glass from cracking.

Decorative garnishes

A party is the perfect occasion for serving drinks with frivolous decorations. Look at the commercial options of pretty straws, paper parasols, indoor sparklers and colourful swizzle sticks, or use thin slices of lemon, orange or lime, sprigs of mint or borage and cocktail (maraschino) cherries. Flower heads and assorted fruits and vegetables – for example slices of kiwi fruit, star fruit, peach, apple, tomato, carrot and cucumber, melon balls, whole strawberries, wedges of pineapple and chunks of banana – also look good. Float the decorations on the drink, twist and skewer them with a cocktail stick or split and hang them on the side of the punch bowl or glass as appropriate.

Citrus rind spirals are another possibility. Using a canelle knife or swivel-headed vegetable peeler, pare from a citrus fruit a long thin strand of rind with a little pith to give it body. Wind the rind around the handle of a wooden spoon to create a spiral then drape it over the side of a glass or the punch bowl.

Stirring, shaking and blending

Clear drinks are normally stirred, while cloudy drinks – those containing egg white, cream, milk, fresh fruit or fruit juices, thick liqueurs and other ingredients that require a very thorough mixing – are shaken or mixed in a blender. Generally, shaken drinks are strained before serving to remove the ice, fragments of fruit or anything that might spoil the appearance of the drink.

Stirring is the simplest way of mixing a drink and requires a mixing glass and a long-handled bar spoon. Simply place your ingredients with ice in the mixing glass, which is generally large enough to mix several drinks at the same time, and stir gently with the spoon. Strain into a glass and serve. Alternatively, simply mix punch ingredients together in a large punch bowl.

Shaking involves placing all the ingredients in a cocktail shaker, together with plenty of cubed or cracked ice, which serves both to chill the drink and to act as a beater in the shaker. Holding the shaker in two hands, shake it vigorously using a quick pumping action until the outside of the shaker is frosty. To avoid a big mess, never shake fizzy ingredients! Made of metal or acrylic, cocktail shakers often come with their own built-in strainer.

Blending involves whizzing all the ingredients, together with crushed or cracked ice, in an electric blender or liquidizer. Never blend carbonated soft drinks or Champagne or your mixture will explode! Add these ingredients only after blending.

Home bar equipment

Depending on the types of drinks you are likely to make, the main items required are a cocktail shaker, a mixing glass and an electric blender. Other bar accessories include double and single bar measures; tongs for ice cubes and a bar strainer to strain drinks; a sifter for sprinkling spices and sugar; a salt saucer, for frosting the rims of glasses. Other essentials are a chopping board and sharp knife, a canelle knife or swivel-headed vegetable peeler for removing citrus rind, a lemon squeezer, ice trays, cocktail sticks, a corkscrew and bottle opener.

Sugar syrup

A non-alcoholic ingredient in many mixed drinks, sugar syrup blends into a cold drink more quickly than sugar and gives it more body. You can buy it ready-made (by the name of gomme syrup), although it is easy to make your own. Simply place 4 tablespoons caster sugar and 4 tablespoons water in a small saucepan. Bring slowly to the boil, stirring to dissolve the sugar, then boil the mixture without stirring for 1–2 minutes. Sugar syrup can be stored in a sterilized bottle in the fridge for up to two months.

Drinks glossary

Bailey's Irish Cream An Irish whiskey and cream liqueur.

Bénédictine A brandy-based liqueur flavoured with herbs, invented by a Norman Bénédictine monk in the early 16th century.

Bitters A powerful herbal or fruit-flavoured essence used in very small quantities to add distinctive flavour to drinks. The original bitters, Angostura, is herb flavoured although details of the recipe are a closely kept secret. Peychaud's bitters is a US brand of bitters invented by Antoine Peychaud in the 18th century.

Bourbon See Whisky

Brandy An alcoholic spirit distilled from wine (ordinary brandy) or fermented fruit (fruit brandies like apricot and cherry brandy).

Cachaça A Brazilian sugar cane brandy.

Chambord Liqueur A French liqueur made from black raspberries.

Champagne Sparkling wine produced by a traditional method in the Champagne region of France. Sparkling wines made elsewhere by the same method are labelled 'Methode Champenoise' and include Cava (from Spain), Spumante (from Italy) and Sekt (from Germany).

Chartreuse A herb-flavoured liqueur created by French Carthusian monks. Green chartreuse is more alcoholic than yellow.

Cider Fermented apple juice, available as strong, dry, medium and sweet.

Coconut cream/milk Commercial products derived from coconut and sold in cans or cartons.

Cointreau A colourless, orange-flavoured brandy-based liqueur.

Crème de bananes A banana-flavoured brandy-based liqueur.

Crème de cacao A chocolate-flavoured liqueur, available in white and brown versions.

Crème de cassis A blackcurrant-flavoured liqueur from France.

Crème de menthe A very sweet peppermint liqueur, which comes in green and colourless versions.

Crème de mure A liqueur made from wild blackberries.

Creole Shrub An orange-flavoured rum from the West Indies.

Curaçao An orange-flavoured liqueur from the Caribbean, available colourless, in blue, orange and green.

Fruit juice Juice extracted from a fresh fruit, or a soft drink made from fruit concentrate, water and sugar. Always use the type of juice specified in the recipe — bottled and carton juices are no substitute for freshly squeezed fruit juice nor vice versa.

Galliano A pale yellow, Italian herb-flavoured liqueur.

Gin A colourless grain spirit flavoured with juniper berries.

Ginger wine A grape-based wine flavoured with ginger, herbs and spices.

Gomme A non-alcoholic syrup made from sugar (see page 9).

Grand Marnier A brandy-based orange liqueur from France.

Grenadine A sweet, red non-alcoholic syrup made from pomegranates.

Kahlúa A coffee-flavoured Mexican liqueur.

Kirsch A colourless fruit brandy distilled from cherries, also known as kirschwasser and cherry schnapps.

Lemon cordial A non-alcoholic lemon syrup.

Liqueurs High-quality spirits flavoured with the flowers, fruits, seeds or leaves of plants, and sweetened with sugar. Known as cordials in the USA.

Maraschino liqueur A liqueur made from black cherries.

Midori A Japanese, bright green, musk melon-flavoured liqueur.

Pernod A French anis-flavoured spirit, which turns pale yellow and cloudy when mixed with water.

Pimm's No. 1 A blend of gin, herb extracts and quinine, invented in 1840 by James Pimm.

Pisang Ambon A sweet, green banana-flavoured liqueur.

Poire William A pear-flavoured brandy.

Rum A spirit distilled from molasses or the fermented juices of sugar cane. Available as white, golden and dark and produced mainly in the West Indies.

Rye See Whisky

Schnapps A strong distilled spirit. Also available flavoured, for example apple, butterscotch, cranberry, lemon, peach, plum and strawberry.

Sherry A fortified wine, available as dry, medium and sweet.

Southern Comfort A US dry liqueur that combines bourbon with peaches, oranges and herbs.

Tequila A colourless Mexican spirit, distilled from the sap of the blue agave cactus.

Tia Maria A Jamaican, rum-based coffee-flavoured liqueur.

Vermouth A fortified wine flavoured with herbs and available as sweet, dry, red and white.

Vodka Traditionally, a colourless grain spirit, it is now available in many flavours, for example blackcurrant, cinnamon, coffee, lemon, mandarin, orange, peach, pepper, raspberry, strawberry and vanilla.

Whisky (Scotch/Canadian) or whiskey (US/Irish) A distillation of grain, malt, sugar and yeast, available in many different varieties. There is no similarity in taste between Scotch, Irish, Canadian or the American whiskies, rye and bourbon.

punches & cups

Gin Cup

Serves 1

3 mint sprigs, plus extra to decorate
1 teaspoon sugar syrup (see page 9)
chopped ice
juice of ½ lemon
3 measures gin

Put the mint and sugar syrup in an old-fashioned glass and stir them about to bruise the mint slightly. Fill the glass with chopped ice, add the lemon juice and gin and stir until a frost begins to form. Decorate with extra mint sprigs.

2

Sangria

Serves 10–12

ice cubes
2 bottles light Spanish red
    wine, chilled
125 ml (4 fl oz) brandy
    (optional)
about 450 ml (¾ pint) soda
    water, chilled
fruit in season, such as
    apples, pears, oranges,
    lemons, peaches and
    strawberries, sliced
orange slices, to decorate

Put the ice in a large bowl
and pour over the wine
and brandy, if using. Stir.
Add soda water to taste
and float the fruit on top.
Serve in tall glasses and
decorate with orange slices.

3

Gage's 'Secret' Sangria

Serves 6

ice cubes
2 measures gin
4 measures Spanish brandy
2 measures orange
    Curaçao
500 ml (17 fl oz) dry red
    wine
500 ml (17 fl oz) lemonade
cinnamon sticks, to stir
apple and orange
    wedges, to decorate

Fill 6 highball glasses with
ice cubes, build the
ingredients in each in the
order given, then decorate
with apple and orange
wedges and serve.

*From the left: Sangria, Gage's
'Secret' Sangria*

4

Brandy and Lemon Sparkler

Serves 15–20

juice of 15 lemons
juice of 4 oranges
625 g (1¼ lb) caster sugar
ice cubes
300 ml (½ pint) orange
    Curaçao
2 measures grenadine
2.5 litres (4 pints) brandy
2.5 litres (4 pints) sparkling
    mineral water
orange and lemon slices, to
    decorate

Pour the lemon and orange juices into a jug. Add the sugar and stir until dissolved. Place a large quantity of ice in a large punch bowl, add all the ingredients and stir well. Decorate with orange and lemon slices.

5

Honeysuckle Cup

Serves 10–12

1 tablespoon clear honey
1 bottle dry white wine
2 tablespoons Bénédictine
150 ml (¼ pint) brandy
750 ml (1¼ pints) lemonade
1 peach, stoned and sliced
fresh raspberries or
    strawberries

Put the honey in a large bowl and gradually stir in the wine. Add the Bénédictine and brandy. Chill for 2 hours. Just before serving, add the lemonade and fruit.

Fish House Punch

600 ml (1 pint) lemon juice
300 g (10 oz) brown sugar
1½ bottles dark rum
¾ bottle brandy
150 ml (¼ pint) peach bitters
1.5 litres (2½ pints) water
2–3 peaches, skinned, stoned and
    roughly chopped
ice cubes

**Serves
15–20**

Put the lemon juice and sugar in
a large punch bowl and stir until
the sugar has dissolved. Add the
rum, brandy, bitters, water and
peaches and stir well to mix.
Chill for about 3 hours, stirring
occasionally. To serve, add ice
cubes to the punch bowl, stir and
ladle into glasses.

punches & cups

7

Boatman's Cup

Serves 14–15

1 bottle Riesling
500 ml (17 fl oz) still dry
　　cider
4 measures brandy
600 ml (1 pint) fresh orange
　　juice
750 ml (1¼ pints) lemonade
black cherries, halved
orange slices
melon balls or cubes
mint sprigs

Mix together the wine,
cider, brandy and orange
juice. Chill for 2 hours. Just
before serving, add the
lemonade, fruit and mint.

8

Bahamas Punch

Serves 4

juice of 4 lemons
4 teaspoons sugar syrup
12 drops Angostura bitters
2 teaspoons grenadine
350 ml (12 fl oz) golden or
　　white rum
4 orange slices
4 lemon slices
cracked ice
grated nutmeg

Pour the lemon juice and
sugar syrup into a mixing
glass. Shake in the bitters,
then add the grenadine,
rum and fruit. Stir and chill.
To serve, fill 4 old-fashioned
glasses with cracked ice,
pour in the punch without
straining and sprinkle each
with nutmeg.

Right: Bahamas Punch

9

Golden Rum Punch

Serves 20

50 g (2 oz) sugar
1 litre (1¾ pints) pineapple juice
juice of 6 oranges
juice of 6 lemons
1 bottle golden rum
ice block
1 litre (1¾ pints) ginger ale or soda water
fruit in season, such as pineapples, oranges, cherries and strawberries, sliced, to decorate

Put the sugar in a punch bowl, pour in the pineapple juice and stir to dissolve the sugar. Add the orange and lemon juices and rum. Stir to mix. Put a large block of ice in the punch bowl and leave the punch to get really cold. When ready to serve, pour in the ginger ale or soda water. Decorate with fruit and serve.

10

Tea Punch

Serves 8

600 ml (1 pint) China tea
125 g (4 oz) sugar
juice of 2 lemons
juice of 1 orange
1 cinnamon stick
150 ml (¼ pint) brandy
150 ml (¼ pint) dark rum
3 measures Grand Marnier
300 ml (½ pint) soda water
orange and lemon slices,
    to decorate

Let the tea infuse, then
strain into a saucepan.
Add the sugar and heat
until dissolved. Add the fruit
juices, cinnamon, brandy
and rum, and heat gently
for 5 minutes. Leave until
cold, then chill for 2 hours.
Add the Grand Marnier,
top up with soda water
and add the fruit.

11

Rose Cup

Serves 12–14

ice cubes
1 bottle sweet white wine
1 bottle pink Champagne,
    chilled
4 tablespoons Southern
    Comfort
450 ml (¾ pint) tonic water
4 tablespoons canned
    mandarin segments

Put the ice in a large
punch bowl and pour in
the wine, Champagne,
Southern Comfort and
tonic water. Add the
mandarin segments, with
their syrup to taste. Serve
as soon as possible.

*From the left: Tea Punch,
Rose Cup*

12

Cranberry Champagne Punch

Serves 16

1 litre (1¾ pints) cranberry juice
250 ml (8 fl oz) brandy
lime wedges
caster sugar, to taste
500 ml (17 fl oz) soda water
1 bottle Champagne

Make sure that all the liquid ingredients are well chilled before mixing them or add some ice cubes to the punch bowl. Combine the cranberry juice, brandy and lime wedges in a punch bowl, stir well and add sugar to taste. Add the soda water and Champagne just before serving.

punches & cups

13

Summer Cup

Serves 12

1 bottle German Riesling, chilled
1 bottle Champagne, chilled
4 measures Grand Marnier
1 dessert apple, cored and sliced
1 orange, sliced
6–10 strawberries, halved
ice cubes
750 ml (1¼ pints) lemonade
mint sprigs, to decorate

Pour the wine, Champagne and liqueur into a chilled punch bowl and add the fruit. To serve, add lots of ice, top up with lemonade and decorate with mint sprigs.

14

Champagne Punch

Serves 15–20

250 g (8 oz) caster sugar
2.5 litres (4 pints) chilled
    Champagne
1.2 litres (2 pints) chilled
    sparkling mineral water
2 measures brandy
2 measures maraschino liqueur
2 measures orange Curaçao
ice cubes
fruit, to decorate

Put all the ingredients in a
large punch bowl containing
plenty of ice cubes and stir
until the sugar has dissolved.
Add fruit to decorate.

punches & cups

15

Roman Punch

**Serves
15–20**

875 g (1¾ lb) sugar
juice of 3 oranges
juice of 10 lemons
1.2 litres (2 pints) Champagne
    or sparkling wine
1.2 litres (2 pints) dark rum
½ measure orange bitters
grated rind of 1 orange
10 egg whites, beaten
ice cubes
orange slices, to decorate

Put the sugar in a large, chilled punch bowl and pour in the orange and lemon juices. Stir gently until the sugar has dissolved. Add the Champagne or sparkling wine, rum, orange bitters, orange rind and the egg whites. Add plenty of ice cubes and stir well. Keep the bowl packed with ice to keep the punch chilled. Decorate with orange slices before serving.

punches & cups

Midsummer Punch

125 g (4 oz) sugar
300 ml (½ pint) water
300 ml (½ pint) fresh
    orange juice
300 ml (½ pint) pineapple juice
600 ml (1 pint) cold weak
    tea, strained
orange, lemon, apple and
    pineapple slices
crushed ice
300 ml (½ pint) ginger ale
mint sprigs, to decorate

Serves 8–10

Put the sugar and water into
a saucepan and stir over a low
heat until the sugar has
dissolved. Leave to cool, then
pour into a large jug or bowl.
Stir in the fruit juices and cold
tea, then add the sliced fruit
and the crushed ice. To serve,
pour into tall glasses and top
up with ginger ale. Decorate
with mint sprigs.

punches & cups

17

Bombay Punch

Serves 25–30

1.2 litres (2 pints) brandy
1.2 litres (2 pints) sherry
150 ml (¼ pint) maraschino liqueur
150 ml (¼ pint) orange Curaçao
5 litres (8 pints) chilled Champagne
2.5 litres (4 pints) sparkling mineral water
ice cubes
fruits and mint sprigs, to decorate

Pour the ingredients into a large punch bowl containing plenty of ice cubes and stir gently. Decorate with fruits in season and mint. Keep the punch bowl packed with ice.

18

Christmas Punch

Serves 15–20

juice of 15 lemons
juice of 4 oranges
625 g (1¼ lb) sugar
ice cubes
300 ml (½ pint) orange
　　Curaçao
2 measures grenadine
2 measures brandy
2.5 litres (4 pints) sparkling
　　mineral water
orange and lemon rind, to
　　decorate

Pour the lemon and orange juices into a jug. Add the sugar and stir gently until it has dissolved. Place a large quantity of ice cubes in a large punch bowl. Add the fruit juices, orange Curaçao, grenadine, brandy and mineral water, and stir well. Decorate with the orange and lemon rind before serving.

Chablis Cup

Serves 6

3 ripe peaches, skinned,
    stoned and sliced
1 orange, thinly sliced
cocktail cherries
3 teaspoons sugar
1 bottle chablis
4 measures Grand Marnier
4 measures kirsch

Put the peaches, orange slices,
cherries and sugar in a punch
bowl. Pour in the chablis,
Grand Marnier and kirsch and
stir thoroughly. Cover the bowl
and chill for 1 hour. Serve in
goblets.

the classics

White Russian

Serves 2

12 cracked ice cubes
2 measures vodka
2 measures Tia Maria
2 measures milk or double
   cream

Put half the ice in a cocktail shaker and add the vodka, Tia Maria and milk or double cream. Shake until a frost forms. Put the remaining ice in 2 tall narrow glasses and strain the cocktail over the ice. Serve with a straw.

Black Russian

Serves 4

cracked ice
8 measures vodka
4 measures Kahlúa
chocolate sticks, to
   decorate (optional)

Put some cracked ice in a mixing glass. Add the vodka and Kahlúa and stir. Pour into 4 short glasses without straining. Decorate each with a chocolate stick, if you like.

the classics

From the left: Black Russian, White Russian

22

Sea Breeze

**Serves
4**

crushed ice
4 measures vodka
6 measures cranberry juice
6 measures fresh grapefruit
    juice
lime slices, to decorate

Put the crushed ice in a mixing
glass, pour over the vodka,
cranberry juice and grapefruit
juice and stir well. Pour into
4 tall glasses. Decorate each
with a lime slice and serve
with straws.

Sex on the Beach

6 ice cubes
1 measure vodka
1 measure peach schnapps
2 measures cranberry juice
2 measures orange juice
2 measures pineapple juice
    (optional)
cocktail cherries, to decorate

Serves 2

Put the ice in a cocktail shaker
and add the vodka, peach
schnapps, cranberry juice, orange
juice and pineapple juice, if using.
Shake until a frost forms. Pour into
2 tall glasses, decorate each with
a cherry and serve with a straw.

the classics

24

Caipirinha

Serves 1

6 lime wedges
2 teaspoons brown sugar
2 measures cachaça or vodka
4–5 ice cubes, crushed

Place 3 of the lime wedges in a large tumbler or old-fashioned glass and add the brown sugar and cachaça or vodka. Mix well, mashing the limes slightly to make a little juice. Top up with the crushed ice and garnish with the remaining lime wedges.

25

Cosmopolitan

Serves 1

ice cubes
1½ measures citron vodka
1 measure Cointreau
1½ measures cranberry juice
¼ measure fresh lime juice
lime wheel, to decorate

Put the ice cubes in a cocktail shaker, add the citron vodka, Cointreau, cranberry juice and lime juice and shake well. Strain into a chilled cocktail glass and add a lime wheel.

the classics

26

Cape Codder

Serves 4

ice cubes
8 measures vodka
400 ml (14 fl oz) cranberry juice
4 limes, each cut into 6
    wedges

Fill a mixing glass with ice cubes, add the vodka and cranberry juice, then squeeze half of the lime wedges into the drink. Stir well, pour into 4 highball glasses and decorate with the remaining lime wedges. Serve each with a straw, if you like.

Vodka Sazerac

1 sugar cube
2 drops Angostura bitters
3 drops Pernod
2–3 ice cubes
2 measures vodka
lemonade, to top up

Serves 1

Put the sugar cube in an old-fashioned glass and shake the bitters on to it. Add the Pernod to the glass and swirl it about so that it clings to the side of the glass. Drop in the ice cubes and pour in the vodka. Top up with lemonade, then stir gently and serve at once with a straw.

the classics

28

Harvey Wallbanger

Serves 1

6 ice cubes
1 measure vodka
125 ml (4 fl oz) fresh orange
    juice
1–2 teaspoons Galliano
orange slices, to decorate

Put half of the ice cubes, the vodka and orange juice in a cocktail shaker. Shake well for about 30 seconds, then strain into a tall glass over the remaining ice cubes. Float the Galliano on top and decorate with orange slices.

29

Moscow Mule

Serves 2

cracked ice
4 measures vodka
juice of 4 limes
ginger beer, to top up
lime slices, to decorate

Put some cracked ice in a cocktail shaker. Add the vodka and lime juice. Shake until a frost forms. Pour into 2 hurricane glasses or large tumblers. Top up with ginger beer. Decorate each with a slice of lime and serve with a straw, if liked.

the classics

30

Dry Martini

Serves 2

ice cubes
1 measure dry vermouth
6 measures gin
2 green olives

Put some ice cubes in a mixing glass. Pour the vermouth and gin over the ice and stir (never shake) vigorously and evenly without splashing, then strain into 2 chilled cocktail glasses. Serve each with a green olive.

31

White Lady

Serves 2

ice cubes
4 measures gin
2 measures Cointreau
2 teaspoons fresh lemon
    juice
about 1 teaspoon egg
    white

Place some ice cubes, the gin, Cointreau, lemon juice and egg white in a cocktail shaker. Shake to mix then strain into 2 chilled cocktail glasses.

the classics

56

Salty Dog

ice cubes
2 pinches of salt
2 measures gin
4–5 measures fresh grapefruit juice
orange slices, to decorate

Serves 2

Put 2–3 ice cubes in each of 2
old-fashioned glasses. Put a pinch
of salt on the ice and add the gin
and grapefruit juice. Stir gently,
decorate each with a slice of
orange and serve.

the classics

33 Long Island Iced Tea

Serves 4

2 measures gin
2 measures vodka
2 measures white rum
2 measures tequila
2 measures Cointreau
3 measures lemon juice
2 teaspoons sugar syrup
(see page 9)
ice cubes
cola
lemon slices and mint
sprigs, to decorate

Pour the first 7 ingredients into a mixing glass and stir thoroughly. Fill 4 tall glass almost full with ice cubes then strain the drink into it. Top each up with cola and decorate with lemon slices and mint sprigs.

34 Silk Stocking

Serves 1

drinking chocolate powder,
for rimming
¾ measure tequila
¾ measure white crème
de cacao
100 ml (3½ fl oz) single
cream
2 teaspoons grenadine
4–5 ice cubes

Dampen the rim of a chilled cocktail glass and dip it into the drinking chocolate powder. Pour the tequila, white crème de cacao, cream and grenadine into a cocktail shaker and add the ice cubes. Shake vigorously for 10 seconds then strain into the chilled cocktail glass.

Right: Silk Stocking

35 Tequila Sunrise

Serves 1

5–6 ice cubes
1 measure tequila
100 ml (3½ fl oz) fresh orange juice
2 teaspoons grenadine
star fruit and orange slices, to decorate

Crack half the ice cubes and put them in a cocktail shaker. Add the tequila and orange juice and shake to mix. Put the remaining ice in a tall glass and strain the tequila mixture into it. Slowly pour in the grenadine and allow it to settle. Just before serving, stir once. Decorate the glass with a star fruit and orange slice.

the classics

60

Margarita

3 measures tequila
2 measures fresh lime juice
2 measures Cointreau
cracked ice
salt, for rimming (optional)
lime slices, to decorate

Serves 2

Put the tequila, lime juice and Cointreau in a cocktail shaker with some cracked ice. Shake thoroughly and strain into 2 cocktail glasses rimmed with salt, if using. Decorate each with a slice of lime.

the classics

Brandy Fix

Serves 6

2 tablespoons powdered
    sugar
2 tablespoons water
6 measures brandy
3 measures cherry brandy
juice of 3 lemons
crushed ice
lemon slices, to decorate

Dissolve the sugar in the
water in a mixing glass then
add the brandy, cherry
brandy and lemon juice.
Stir to mix. Pour into 6
brandy balloons or small
tumblers. Fill the glasses
with crushed ice, float a
lemon slice on top of each
and serve with a straw.

Metropolitan

Serves 2

2 measures brandy
2 measures sweet
    vermouth
1 teaspoon sugar syrup
    (see page 9)
6–8 dashes Angostura
    bitters
cracked ice

Put the brandy, vermouth,
sugar syrup and bitters in a
cocktail shaker with some
cracked ice and shake
well. Strain into 2 chilled
cocktail glasses.

Right: Brandy Fix

Brandy Sour

Serves 1

4–5 ice cubes
3 drops Angostura bitters
juice of 1 lemon
3 measures brandy
1 teaspoon sugar syrup
    (see page 9)
lemon slices, to decorate

Put the ice cubes in a
cocktail shaker. Shake the
bitters over the ice, add the
lemon juice, brandy and
sugar syrup and shake until
a frost forms. Strain into a
tumbler and decorate with
lemon slices on a cocktail
stick. Serve with a straw.

Brandy Manhattan

Serves 4

ice cubes
4 measures sweet
    vermouth
12 measures brandy
cocktail cherries, to
    decorate

Put the ice cubes in a
mixing glass. Pour the
vermouth and brandy over
the ice and stir vigorously.
Pour into 4 chilled glasses
and decorate each with a
cocktail cherry.

Right: Brandy Manhattan

the classics

41

Mai Tai

Serves 2

lightly beaten egg white and caster sugar, for rimming
2 measures white rum
1 measure fresh orange juice
1 measure fresh lime juice
crushed ice
cocktail cherries, pineapple cubes and orange slices, to decorate

Dip the rim of 2 tall glasses into the beaten egg white, then in the caster sugar. Put the rum, orange juice and lime juice in a cocktail shaker. Shake to mix. Put some crushed ice in the sugar-rimmed glasses and pour the cocktail over it. Decorate with the cherries, pineapple and slices of orange and serve with a straw.

the classics

66

42

Zombie

Serves 1

cracked ice cubes
1 measure dark rum
1 measure white rum
½ measure apricot brandy
2 measures pineapple juice
1 tablespoon fresh lime juice
2 teaspoons powdered sugar
cocktail cherry, pineapple
 wedge and mint sprig, to
 decorate

Place a hurricane glass in
the freezer until the outside
becomes frosted. Put the ice
in a cocktail shaker, add the
rums, apricot brandy, fruit juices
and sugar. Shake to mix. Pour
into the glass without straining.
To decorate, spear the cherry
and pineapple on a cocktail
stick and place across the top
of the glass, Add the mint sprig
and serve with a straw.

Cuba Libre

Serves 4

ice cubes
6 measures dark rum
juice of 2 limes
cola, to top up
lime slices, to decorate

Place 2–3 ice cubes in
each of 4 tall tumblers and
pour over one-quarter of
the rum and lime juice. Stir
to mix. Top up with cola,
decorate each with a lime
slice and a straw.

Piña Colada

Serves 2

4 measures white rum
4 measures coconut milk
4 measures pineapple juice
crushed ice
pineapple wedges, to
    decorate

Put the rum, coconut milk
and pineapple juice in a
blender with some crushed
ice and blend until slushy.
Serve in hurricane glasses
and decorate with
pineapple wedges.

the classics

45

Rum Crusta

Serves
1

lime wedge and caster sugar,
  for rimming
2 measures dark rum
1 measure Cointreau
2 teaspoons maraschino
  liqueur
2 teaspoons fresh lime juice
ice cubes
crushed ice
2 grapes, to decorate

Moisten the rim of an old-
fashioned glass with the lime
wedge and dip it in caster
sugar. Put the rum, Cointreau,
maraschino liqueur and lime
juice in a cocktail shaker with
some ice cubes and mix well.
Strain into an old-fashioned
glass filled with crushed ice
and decorate with the grapes.

Daiquiri

Serves 1

cracked ice
juice of 2 limes
1 teaspoon sugar syrup
   (see page 9)
3 measures white rum
lime wheel, to decorate

Put lots of cracked ice in
a cocktail shaker. Pour the
lime juice, sugar syrup and
rum over the ice. Shake
thoroughly, then strain into
a chilled cocktail glass
and decorate with the
lime wheel.

Frozen Pineapple Daiquiri

Serves 4

crushed ice
10 pineapple slices
2 measure fresh lime juice
4 measures white rum
1 measure Cointreau
4 teaspoons sugar syrup
   (see page 9)
pineapple wedges, to
   decorate

Put some crushed ice in a
blender and add the
pineapple slices, lime juice,
white rum, Cointreau and
sugar syrup. Blend until
smooth, then pour into 4
chilled cocktail glasses.
Decorate with fresh
pineapple and serve.

Right: Frozen Pineapple Daiquiri

the classics

48

Rhett Butler

Serves 1

2 measures bourbon whiskey
100 ml (4 fl oz) cranberry juice
2 tablespoons sugar syrup (see page 9)
1 tablespoon fresh lime juice
ice cubes
lime slices, to decorate

Put the bourbon, cranberry juice, sugar syrup and lime juice in a cocktail shaker with some ice cubes and mix well. Fill an old-fashioned glass with fresh ice cubes and strain the cocktail into it. Decorate with lime slices.

Manhattan

8 measures rye or bourbon
    whiskey
4 measures extra-dry vermouth
16 dashes Angostura bitters
ice cubes
cocktail cherries, to decorate

Serves 4

Put the whiskey, vermouth and
bitters in a mixing glass with some
ice cubes and stir. Strain into 4
chilled cocktail glasses. Decorate
each with a cocktail cherry.

the classics

50

Whisky Daisy

Serves 2

crushed ice
2 egg whites (optional)
1 measure fresh lemon juice
2 measures Scotch whisky
2 teaspoons Pernod
4 dashes grenadine
soda water, to top up
lemon rind spirals, to decorate

Put the ice in a cocktail shaker and add the egg white, if using, the lemon juice, whisky, Pernod and grenadine. Shake to mix. Pour into 2 tumblers, top up with soda water and decorate each with a lemon rind spiral.

sparklers

51

Martini Royale

Serves 4

10 measures frozen vodka
1 measure crème de cassis
chilled Champagne, to top up
lemon rind spiral, to decorate

Pour 2½ measures of the
vodka into each of 4 chilled
cocktail glasses then stir in ¼
measure of cassis. Top up
with Champagne then add
a lemon twist to each.

52 Singapore Gin Sling

Serves 1

6–8 ice cubes
juice of ½ lemon
juice of ½ orange
1 measure cherry brandy
3 measures gin
3 drops Angostura bitters
soda water, to top up
lemon slice, to decorate

Put 4–6 ice cubes in a cocktail shaker. Pour the lemon and orange juices, cherry brandy and gin over the ice and add the bitters. Shake the mixture until a frost forms. Put 2 fresh ice cubes in a hurricane glass. Strain the cocktail into the glass and top up with soda water. Decorate with the lemon slice and serve.

53

Harlequin

Serves 2

lightly beaten egg white and
caster sugar, for rimming
2 measures kirsch
2 measures apricot brandy
4 measures orange juice
soda water, to top up
orange slices and cocktail
cherries, to decorate

Dip the rim of 2 tumblers in
the lightly beaten egg white,
then in caster sugar. Place the
kirsch, apricot brandy and
orange juice in a cocktail
shaker. Shake lightly. Strain
into the glasses and top up
with soda water. Decorate
each glass with an orange
slice and 2 cherries.

54 Celebration Cocktail

Serves 4

4 lemon wedges and caster
    sugar, for rimming
ice cubes
4 measures brandy
4 dashes Bénédictine
4 dashes crème de mure
chilled Champagne, to top up

Frost the rim of 4 Champagne
flutes using the lemon wedges
and sugar. Put the ice in a
cocktail shaker and add the
brandy, Bénédictine and
crème de mure. Shake well,
strain into the flutes and top up
with Champagne.

55 New Orleans Dandy

Serves 4

crushed ice
4 measures light rum
2 measures peach brandy
4 dashes orange juice
4 dashes fresh lime juice
chilled Champagne, to top up

Place the crushed ice in a cocktail shaker with the rum, peach brandy, orange juice and lime juice. Shake until a frost forms. Strain into 4 large wine glasses and top up with Champagne.

sparklers

Hummingbird

4–5 ice cubes, crushed
1 measure dark rum
1 measure light rum
1 measure Southern Comfort
1 measure fresh orange juice
cola, to top up
orange slices, to decorate

Serves 1

Put the crushed ice in a cocktail
shaker. Pour the dark and light
rums, Southern Comfort and
orange juice over the ice and
shake until a frost forms. Strain into
a long glass and top up with cola.
Decorate with a slice of orange
and serve with a straw.

sparklers

57

Pink Rum

Serves 4

12 drops Angostura bitters
ice cubes
8 measures white rum
8 measures cranberry juice
4 measures soda water
lime slices, to decorate

Shake 3 drops of bitters into each of 4 highball glasses and swirl them around. Add 3–4 ice cubes to each glass, then pour in the white rum, cranberry juice and soda water and serve each decorated with a lime slice.

58 Caribbean Champagne

Serves 4

400 ml (14 fl oz) light rum
1 measure crème de bananes
4 dashes Angostura bitters
chilled Champagne or
   sparkling dry white wine, to
   top up
banana slices, pineapple
   chunks and cocktail
   cherries, to decorate

Pour 100 ml (3 fl oz) rum, ¼ measure crème de bananes and a dash of Angostura bitters into each of 4 Champagne glasses. Top up with Champagne or sparkling white wine, and stir gently. Decorate each with a slice of banana, pineapple and a cherry, all speared on a cocktail stick.

sparklers

59 Raspberry Champagne Cocktail

Serves 6

125 g (4 oz) fresh raspberries
3 tablespoons crème de cassis
1 bottle Champagne, chilled
4–6 teaspoons grenadine
(optional)

Put the raspberries in a small bowl with the crème de cassis and leave to macerate for at least 30 minutes. Divide the raspberries between 6 Champagne flutes and top up with chilled Champagne. Add grenadine to taste, if using, and serve immediately.

60 California Dreaming

Serves 2

crushed ice
4 dashes kirsch
6 measures pineapple juice
2 dashes of lemon juice
chilled Champagne, to top up
pineapple slices, to decorate

Put some crushed ice in a cocktail shaker. Pour in the kirsch and fruit juices, and shake for 45 seconds. Pour into 2 glasses and top up with Champagne. Decorate with pineapple slices.

sparklers

Millennium Cocktail

ice cubes
2 measures vodka
2 measures fresh raspberry juice
2 measures orange juice
8 measures chilled Champagne

Serves 2

Put some ice cubes in a cocktail shaker, add the vodka, raspberry juice and orange juice and shake thoroughly. Strain into 2 Champagne flutes and pour in the chilled Champagne.

sparklers

62

Mango Bellini

Serves 6–8

600 ml (1 pint) mango
    juice
chilled pink Champagne,
    to top up

Divide the mango juice
between 6–8 Champagne
flutes and top up with
Champagne. Stir gently to
mix and serve immediately.

63

Peach and Elderflower Bellini

Serves 6

2 ripe peaches
4 tablespoons elderflower
    cordial
1 bottle Champagne,
    chilled
elderflowers, to decorate

Plunge the peaches into
boiling water for 1–2
minutes. Refresh under
cold water and peel off
the skins. Halve, stone and
chop the flesh. Process the
peaches and elderflower
cordial in a food processor
to a fairly smooth purée.
Divide the purée between
6 glasses. Top up with
Champagne and
decorate with elderflowers.

Right: Mango Bellini

64

Classic Champagne Cocktail

Serves 6

6 sugar cubes
6–12 dashes Angostura
    bitters
6 measures brandy
chilled Champagne, to
    top up
orange slices, to decorate

Put a sugar cube in each
of 6 chilled cocktail or
Champagne glasses and
saturate with 1–2 dashes of
bitters. Add a measure of
brandy to each, then fill the
glass with Champagne.
Decorate each with a slice
of orange.

65

The Classic's Classic

Serves 6

6 sugar cubes
12 dashes Angostura bitters
6 measures Grand Marnier
chilled Champagne, to
    top up
orange rind, to decorate

Saturate each sugar cube
with the bitters then drop
it into a Champagne flute.
Add a measure of Grand
Marnier then top up with
the chilled Champagne.
Place a piece of orange
rind in each drink to
decorate.

*Right: Classic Champagne
Cocktail*

Americana

Serves 6

3 teaspoons sugar
6 measures bourbon whisky
6 dashes Angostura bitters
chilled Champagne, to top up
peach slices, to decorate

Dissolve ½ teaspoon sugar in a measure of bourbon in each of 6 wide Champagne glasses. Stir in a dash of Angostura bitters. Top up each glass with Champagne and decorate with a peach slice.

Tequila Slammer

6 measures tequila gold
6 measures chilled Champagne

Serves 6

Take 6 shot glasses. Pour a measure
of tequila into each shot glass.
Slowly top up with Champagne.
To drink, cover the top of the glass
with the palm of your hand to seal
the contents inside and grip it with
your fingers. Briskly pick up the
glass and slam it down on to a
surface to make the drink fizz then
quickly gulp it down in one, while
it is still fizzing.

sparklers

103

68

Grand Mimosa

Serves 6

6 measures Grand Marnier
12 measures chilled
    orange juice
chilled Champagne, to
    top up

Pour a measure of Grand Marnier and 2 of orange juice into each of 6 Champagne flutes. Top up with chilled Champagne and serve.

69

Grandaddy Mimosa

Serves 2

2 measures Havana Club
    3-year-old rum
2 measures orange juice
2 tablespoons lemon juice
ice cubes
chilled Champagne, to
    top up
orange rind spirals, to
    decorate
2 dashes grenadine

Put the rum, orange and lemon juice into a cocktail shaker with some ice cubes and shake. Strain into 2 large Champagne flutes then top up with chilled Champagne. Decorate each with an orange rind spiral, and drop in the grenadine.

From the left: Grand Mimosa, Grandaddy Mimosa

70

Ritz Fizz

Serves 6

6 dashes blue Curaçao
6 dashes lemon juice
6 dashes Amaretto di Saronno
chilled Champagne, to top up
lemon rind spirals, to decorate

Pour a dash each of Curaçao, lemon juice and Amaretto into 6 glasses and top up each with Champagne. Stir gently to mix and decorate the glasses with lemon rind spirals.

71

Melon Ball

Serves 2

cracked ice
2 measures vodka
2 measures Midori
2 measures orange juice, plus
    extra to top up
orange slices and small
    banana balls, to decorate

Put some cracked ice in each
of 2 tall glasses or goblets. Pour
the vodka, Midori and orange
juice into a cocktail shaker.
Shake well to mix, then strain
into the glasses. Top up
with more orange juice if
necessary. Decorate with the
fruit and serve with a straw.

72

Iced Lemon and Mint Vodka

Serves 6

4 tablespoons lemon juice
125 ml (4 fl oz) lemon
    cordial
125 ml (4 fl oz) chilled
    vodka
ice cubes
tonic water, to top up
a few mint sprigs, to
    decorate

Pour the lemon juice, lemon cordial and chilled vodka into a cocktail shaker and shake well. Pour into 6 tall glasses half-filled with ice cubes. Top up with tonic water, add a few mint sprigs and serve immediately.

73

Siamese Slammer

Serves 4

3 measures vodka
juice of 2 oranges
1 small ripe papaya,
    peeled and chopped
1 banana, sliced
juice of 1 lime
3 measures sugar syrup
8 ice cubes, crushed
4 papaya slices, to
    decorate

Put all the ingredients in a blender and blend until smooth. Serve in 4 tall glasses, each decorated with a slice of papaya.

Right: Iced Lemon and Mint Vodka

74

Snapdragon

Serves 4

ice cubes
8 measures vodka
475 ml (16 fl oz) green crème
    de menthe
soda water, to top up
mint sprigs, to decorate

Fill 4 highball glasses with ice
cubes. Divide the vodka and
crème de menthe among the
glasses and stir. Top up with
soda water. Decorate each
drink with a mint sprig.

75

Gin Tropical

Serves 1

4–6 ice cubes
1½ measures gin
1 measure fresh lemon
    juice
1 measure passion fruit
    juice
½ measure fresh orange
    juice
soda water, to top up
orange rind spiral, to
    decorate

Put half the ice in a
cocktail shaker, pour in the
gin, lemon juice, passion
fruit juice and orange juice
and shake well. Put the
remaining ice in an old-
fashioned glass and strain
in the cocktail. Top up with
soda water and stir gently.
Decorate with an orange
rind spiral.

76

Honolulu

Serves 1

4–5 ice cubes
1 measure pineapple juice
1 measure fresh lemon
    juice
1 measure fresh orange
    juice
½ teaspoon grenadine
3 measures gin
pineapple slice and
    cocktail cherry, to
    decorate

Put the ice cubes in a
cocktail shaker. Pour the
pineapple, lemon and
orange juices, the
grenadine and gin over the
ice and shake until a frost
forms. Strain the drink into a
chilled cocktail glass and
decorate with the
pineapple and cherry.

Right: Gin Tropical

77

Lime Gin Fizz

Serves 1

4–5 ice cubes
2 measures gin
1 measure lime cordial
soda water
lime wedges, to decorate

Put the ice cubes into a tall glass. Pour the gin and the lime cordial over the ice cubes. Top up with soda water, decorate with wedges of lime and serve with straws.

Maiden's Prayer

ice cubes
6 drops Angostura bitters
juice of 2 lemons
2 measures Cointreau
4 measures gin

Serves 2

Put the ice cubes in a cocktail
shaker. Pour the bitters over
the ice, add the lemon juice,
Cointreau and gin and shake until
a frost forms. Strain into 2 cocktail
glasses and serve with a straw.

summer

79

Alice Springs

Serves 1

4–5 ice cubes
1 measure fresh lemon juice
1 measure fresh orange juice
½ teaspoon grenadine
3 measures gin
3 drops Angostura bitters
soda water, to top up
orange slice, to decorate

Put the ice cubes in a cocktail
shaker. Pour in the lemon juice,
orange juice, grenadine and
gin. Add the bitters and shake
until a frost forms. Pour into a
tall glass and top up with soda
water. Decorate with a slice of
orange and serve with straws.

Maracuja

Serves 1

1 fresh ripe passion fruit
1¼ measures tequila gold
1 tablespoon Creole Shrub
¾ measure fresh lime juice
2 teaspoons Cointreau
1 teaspoon passion fruit
    syrup
4–5 ice cubes
physalis (Cape
    gooseberry), to
    decorate

Cut the passion fruit in half
and scoop the flesh into a
cocktail shaker. Add the
tequila, Creole Shrub, lime
juice, Cointreau, passion
fruit syrup and ice cubes
and shake vigorously for
10 seconds. Strain through
a small fine sieve into a
chilled cocktail glass.
Decorate with a physalis.

Cobalt Margarita

Serves 1

1 lime wedge and fine sea
    salt, for rimming
1¼ measures tequila
2 teaspoons Cointreau
½ measure blue Curaçao
¾ measure fresh lime juice
¾ measure fresh grapefruit
    juice
4–5 ice cubes
lime rind spiral, to decorate

Dampen the rim of a
chilled cocktail glass with
a lime wedge then dip it
into fine sea salt. Pour the
remaining ingredients into
a cocktail shaker and
shake vigorously for 10
seconds then strain into the
cocktail glass. Decorate
with a lime rind spiral.

Right: Cobalt Margarita

Tijuana Sling

Serves 2

2½ measures tequila
1½ measures crème de cassis
1½ measures fresh lime juice
4 dashes Peychaud bitters
ice cubes
200 ml (7 fl oz) ginger ale
lime wheels and fresh
    blackcurrants or blueberries,
    to decorate

Pour the tequila, crème
de cassis, lime juice and
Peychaud bitters into a
cocktail shaker. Add the ice
cubes and shake vigorously.
Pour into 2 350 ml (12 fl oz) sling
glasses then top up with ginger
ale. Decorate each glass with
a lime wheel and fresh berries.

83

Texas Tea

Serves 1

¾ measure tequila
1 tablespoon white rum
1 tablespoon Cointreau
2 teaspoons sugar syrup (see page 9)
¾ measure fresh lemon juice
¾ measure fresh orange juice
100 ml (3½ fl oz) strong fruit tea, chilled
ice cubes
orange and lemon slices and mint sprig, to decorate

Pour the tequila, rum, Cointreau, sugar syrup, lemon juice, orange juice and tea into a cocktail shaker, add a handful of ice cubes and shake vigorously. Fill a 350 ml (12 fl oz) sling glass with fresh ice cubes and strain the drink over them. Decorate with orange and lemon slices and a mint sprig.

Brooklyn Bomber

10 ice cubes, crushed
1 measure tequila
1 measure Curaçao
1 measure cherry brandy
1 measure Galliano
2 measures lemon juice
orange slices and cocktail
    cherries, to decorate

Serves 2

Put half the ice cubes in a
cocktail shaker and add the
tequila, Curaçao, cherry brandy,
Galliano and lemon juice. Shake
to mix. Put the remaining ice in 2
hurricane glasses or tall glasses
and pour the drink over it.
Decorate each with a slice of
orange and 2 cherries and serve
with a straw.

summer

85

Acapulco Bliss

Serves 1

¾ measure tequila
1 tablespoon Pisang Ambon
    (banana liqueur)
2 teaspoons Galliano
¾ measure fresh lemon juice
¾ measure single cream
100 ml (3½ fl oz) passion fruit
    juice
4–5 ice cubes
lemon slices, pineapple
    wedges and mint sprig, to
    decorate

Pour the tequila, Pisang
Ambon, Galliano, lemon juice,
cream and passion fruit juice
into a cocktail shaker. Add
the ice cubes and shake
vigorously. Pour into a 350 ml
(12 fl oz) sling glass and
decorate with lemon slices,
a pineapple wedge and a
mint sprig.

86 Brandy Cuban

Serves 4

ice cubes
6 measures brandy
juice of 2 limes
cola, to top up
lime slices, to decorate

Place some ice cubes in each of 4 tumblers and pour over the brandy and lime juice. Stir vigorously to mix. Top up with cola and decorate each glass with a slice of lime. Serve with a straw.

87

East India

Serves 4

ice cubes
12 drops Angostura bitters
2 measures pineapple juice
2 measures blue Curaçao
8 measures brandy
orange rind spiral, to decorate

Put the ice cubes in a mixing glass. Shake the bitters over the ice and add the pineapple juice, Curaçao and brandy. Stir until frothy, then strain into 4 chilled cocktail glasses. Decorate each with a spiral of orange rind tied into a knot.

Frozen Alexander

Serves 4

4 measures brandy
4 measures brown crème
    de cacao
4 scoops vanilla ice-cream
cracked ice
drinking chocolate powder,
    to decorate

Place the first 3 ingredients
in a food processor and
process together. Pour
into 4 ice-filled glasses
and sprinkle with drinking
chocolate powder.

Frozen Apricot Sour

Serves 2

4 measures apricot brandy
2 measures lemon juice
2 scoops vanilla ice-cream
cracked ice

Place the first 3 ingredients
in a food processor and
process together. Pour into
2 ice-filled glasses and
serve.

Right: Frozen Alexander

90 Tropical Dream

Serves 1

1 measure white rum
1 measure Midori
1 tablespoon coconut cream
1 tablespoon pineapple juice
3 tablespoons fresh orange juice
3–4 ice cubes
½ measure crème de bananes
½ fresh banana
fresh banana wedge, with skin on, to decorate

Pour the white rum, Midori, coconut cream, pineapple juice, orange juice and the ice cubes into a blender. Blend for about 10 seconds. Add the crème de bananes and the fresh banana and blend for a further 10 seconds. Pour into a tall glass and decorate with the wedge of banana and serve with a straw.

91

St Lucia

Serves 1

4–5 ice cubes
1 measure Curaçao
1 measure dry vermouth
juice of ½ orange
1 teaspoon grenadine
2 measures white or
    golden rum
orange rind spiral and
    cocktail cherry, to
    decorate

Put the ice cubes in a
cocktail shaker. Pour the
Curaçao, dry vermouth,
orange juice, grenadine
and rum over the ice.
Shake until a frost forms,
then pour, without straining,
into a highball glass.
Decorate with an orange
rind spiral and a cocktail
cherry.

92

Blue Hawaiian

Serves 2

crushed ice
2 measures white rum
1 measure blue Curaçao
4 measures pineapple juice
2 measures coconut cream
pineapple wedges, to
    decorate

Put some crushed ice in a
blender and pour in the
rum, blue Curaçao,
pineapple juice and
coconut cream. Blend at
high speed for 20–30
seconds. Pour into 2 chilled
cocktail glasses and
decorate each with a
pineapple wedge.

Right: St Lucia

Benedict

Serves 4

ice cubes
4 measures Bénédictine
12 measures Scotch whisky
dry ginger ale, to top up

Put some ice cubes in a mixing
glass. Pour the Bénédictine
and whisky over the ice. Stir
evenly without splashing then,
without straining, pour the
cocktail into 4 chilled highball
glasses. Top up with dry ginger
ale and serve.

94

Virginia Mint Julep

Serves 1

9 tender young mint sprigs, plus
  extra to decorate
1 teaspoon sugar syrup (see
  page 9)
crushed ice
3 measures bourbon whiskey

Put the mint sprigs in an iced
silver mug or tall glass. Add the
sugar syrup, then crush the
mint into the syrup with a long
teaspoon. Fill the mug or glass
with crushed ice, pour the
bourbon over the ice and stir
gently. Pack in more crushed
ice and stir until a frost forms.
Wrap the mug or glass in a
table napkin and serve
decorated with a mint sprig.

95

Grasshopper

Serves 4

4 measures green crème de
    menthe
4 measures crème de cacao
4 measures double or
    whipping cream
ice cubes

Put all the ingredients in a
cocktail shaker. Shake well
then strain into 4 glasses.

Classic Pimm's

250 ml (8 fl oz) Pimm's No. 1
ice cubes
orange, lemon and cucumber
    slices
400 ml (14 fl oz) lemonade
mint or borage sprigs, to decorate

Serves 4

Pour the Pimm's into a large glass jug and add ice cubes and the fruit and cucumber slices, then pour in the lemonade. Serve in highball glasses decorated with mint or borage sprigs.

summer

winter warmers

Glögg

Serves 8–10

125 g (4 oz) sugar
1 bottle brandy
12 cloves
pinch of ground cinnamon
pinch of grated nutmeg
40 g (1½ oz) large raisins
40 g (1½ oz) unsalted blanched almonds
900 ml (1½ pints) medium sweet sherry

Put the sugar in a saucepan. Pour in the brandy and stir gently until the sugar has dissolved. Add the cloves, cinnamon, nutmeg, raisins and almonds, and heat to just below simmering point for 10 minutes. Heat the sherry separately to just below simmering point. Ignite the spicy brandy mixture and pour in the hot sherry. Serve immediately in warmed glasses or mugs.

Glühwein

1 lemon
8 cloves
1 bottle red wine
125 g (4 oz) sugar
2 x 5 cm (2-inch) cinnamon sticks
475 ml (16 fl oz) brandy

Serves 6

Spike the lemon with the cloves.
Put the lemon, red wine, sugar
and cinnamon sticks into a
saucepan and heat to just below
simmering point for 10 minutes.
Reduce the heat and add the
brandy. Warm gently for 2–3
minutes. Remove the lemon from
the pan. Strain the liquid and
serve immediately in warmed
glasses or mugs.

winter warmers

149

99

Coffee Diablo

Serves 4

hot black filter coffee
4 measures brandy
2 measures Cointreau
8 cloves
4 pieces of orange rind
4 pieces of lemon rind

Make enough hot black coffee to fill 4 heatproof glasses three-quarters full. Pour the brandy and Cointreau into a small saucepan and add the cloves and orange and lemon rind. Place the pan over a low heat. Just before the mixture comes to the boil, light it with a long taper and pour the flaming mixture over the coffee. Serve at once.

100

Hot Toddy Supreme

Serves 4

8 measures Stone's
   ginger wine
4 measures brandy
4 tablespoons double cream
4 cinnamon sticks
2 teaspoons grated
   orange rind

Gently heat the ginger wine
and brandy in a saucepan to
just below boiling point. Pour
into 4 warmed cups or glasses
and gently pour a tablespoon
of cream over the back of a
warm spoon on to the surface
of each. Add the cinnamon
sticks and sprinkle the orange
rind over the top to decorate.

Hot Brandy Punch

grated rind and juice of 2 lemons
10 cm (4 inch) cinnamon stick
generous grating of nutmeg
6 cloves
6 tablespoons sugar syrup (see
     page 9)
300 ml (½ pint) boiling water
1 bottle brandy

**Serves
8–10**

Put the lemon rind, cinnamon,
nutmeg, cloves, sugar syrup and
boiling water into a saucepan
and simmer for 10 minutes. Strain
into a warmed heatproof punch
bowl and add the lemon juice
and brandy. Set the punch alight
and ladle into warmed mugs.

winter warmers

102

Mulled Ale

Serves 12

1.2 litres (2 pints) brown ale
150 ml (¼ pint) brandy
3 tablespoons brown sugar
6 cloves
1 teaspoon ground ginger
pinch of grated nutmeg
pinch of ground cinnamon
thinly peeled rind and juice
    of 1 lemon
thinly peeled rind and juice
    of 1 orange
600 ml (1 pint) water
orange slices, to decorate

Put all the ingredients in a large saucepan. Bring slowly to the boil, stirring all the time to dissolve the sugar. Turn off the heat and leave to stand for a few minutes. To serve, strain into warmed mugs and float orange slices on top.

103 Island Cream Grog

Serves 2

4 measures rum
400 ml (14 fl oz) boiling water
sugar, to taste
4 tablespoons double cream
grated nutmeg, to decorate

Warm 2 heatproof glasses with a handle and pour in the rum and boiling water. Add sugar to taste and stir. Pour the cream over the back of a warm teaspoon on to the surface of the hot drink and sprinkle with grated nutmeg, to serve.

104

Sunset Tea

Serves 4

400 ml (14 fl oz) freshly brewed
    Indian tea
1 measure golden rum
2 measures Cointreau
4 measures orange juice
2 orange slices, each stuck
    with 3 cloves and cinnamon
    sticks, to decorate

Pour the tea into 4 heatproof
glasses. Put the rum, Cointreau
and orange juice in a small
saucepan. Place it over a low
heat and bring the mixture to
just under boiling point stirring
constantly. Pour immediately
into the glasses with the tea.
Decorate each one with a
slice of orange stuck with 3
cloves, and a cinnamon stick.

winter warmers

105

Fruit Punch

Serves 6

600 ml (1 pint) orange juice
600 ml (1 pint) apple juice
150 ml (¼ pint) water
½ teaspoon ground ginger
½ teaspoon mixed spice
brown or white sugar, to
    taste (optional)
6 measures whisky
1 apple, thinly sliced, to
    decorate

Place the orange and
apple juices, water and
spices in a saucepan and
bring gently to the boil,
adding sugar to taste if
required. Simmer the
mixture for 5 minutes then
stir in the whisky. Pour the
punch into a warmed bowl
and float the apple slices
on top.

106

Heartwarmer

Serves 10–12

200 ml (7 fl oz) red grape
    juice
250 g (8 oz) brown sugar
350 ml (12 fl oz) dark rum
1.5 litres (2½ pints) dry
    white wine
450 ml (¾ pint) red wine

Put the grape juice in a
saucepan, add the sugar
and stir over a gentle heat
until the sugar has dissolved
completely. Stir in the dark
rum and set aside. Pour the
white wine and red wine
into a large saucepan and
heat until hot, but not
boiling. Add the rum and
grape juice mixture and stir
together. Serve hot.

Right: Fruit Punch

107

Irish Coffee

Serves 4

hot black filter coffee
4 measures Irish whiskey
6 tablespoons lightly whipped
    cream
sprinkle of ground coffee, to
    decorate

Make enough hot black
coffee for 8 people. Place a
bar spoon in each of 4 large
wine glasses, add a measure
of whiskey, then top up with
coffee and stir. Heat the cream
very slightly then pour over the
back of a spoon on to the
surface of the coffee to get a
good float. Decorate with a
pinch of ground coffee.

Mulled Wine

150 ml (¼ pint) water
8 cloves
2 x 10 cm (4 inch) cinnamon sticks
1 tablespoon brown sugar
1 lemon, thinly sliced
1 bottle red wine
150 ml (¼ pint) port (optional)

Serves 6

Put the water, cloves, cinnamon sticks and sugar in a large saucepan and boil for 5 minutes. Add the lemon slices then remove the pan from the heat and leave to infuse for 10 minutes. Add the wine and heat slowly for 5 minutes, to just below simmering point. Add the port, if using, and serve hot, in warmed heatproof glasses or mugs.

winter warmers

109

Mexican Marshmallow Mocha

Serves 4

8 teaspoons cocoa
    powder, plus extra to
    decorate
4 measures Kahlúa
400 ml (14 fl oz) hot black
    filter coffee
mini marshmallows and
    whipped cream, to float

Put 2 teaspoons cocoa
powder in each of 4 toddy
glasses, add a measure of
Kahlúa and the coffee
and stir until mixed. Drop in
the mini marshmallows and
float the cream on top.
Decorate with extra cocoa
powder.

110

Spiced Ginger Punch

Serves 12

2 oranges, studded with
    cloves, to taste
1 cm (½ inch) piece of
    fresh root ginger, peeled
    and grated
2 litres (3½ pints) ginger ale
10 cm (4 inch) cinnamon
    stick

Bake the clove-studded
oranges in a preheated
oven at 180°C (350°F), Gas
Mark 4, for 25 minutes, until
golden. Slice, then put in a
saucepan with the ginger,
ginger ale and cinnamon.
Bring to boiling point, but
do not boil. Remove the
cinnamon then serve in
heatproof glasses.

Right: Spiced Ginger Punch

exciting & unusual

Haven

Serves 4

ice cubes
4 tablespoons grenadine
4 measures Pernod
4 measures vodka
soda water, to top up

Put 2–3 ice cubes in each of 4 old-fashioned glasses. Dash the grenadine over the ice, then pour in the Pernod and vodka. Top up with soda water.

112

Sex in the Dunes

Serves 2

2 measures vodka
2 measures peach schnapps
1 measure Chambord liqueur
2 measures pineapple juice
ice cubes
pineapple strips, to decorate

Put the vodka, schnapps, Chambord and pineapple juice in a cocktail shaker with some ice cubes and shake until the outside of the shaker becomes frosted. Strain into 2 old-fashioned glasses filled with ice. Decorate with pineapple strips.

The Bed Taker

4 measures Midori
4 measures vodka
4 measures orange juice
12 chunks of ripe galia melon
crushed ice
melon slices, to decorate

Serves 4

Put the Midori, vodka, orange juice, melon and some crushed ice into a blender and blend until slushy. Pour into 4 large brandy balloons and decorate with melon slices.

exciting & unusual

171

114

Playa Del Mar

Serves 1

1 orange slice and light brown sugar and sea salt mixture, for rimming
ice cubes
1¼ measures tequila gold
¾ measure Grand Marnier
2 teaspoons fresh lime juice
¾ measure cranberry juice
¾ measure pineapple juice
pineapple wedge and orange rind spiral, to decorate

Dampen the rim of a sling glass with the orange slice then dip it into the brown sugar and sea salt mixture. Fill the glass with ice cubes. Pour the tequila, Grand Marnier, lime juice, cranberry juice and pineapple juice into a cocktail shaker. Fill the shaker with ice cubes and shake vigorously for 10 seconds then strain into the sling glass. Decorate with a pineapple wedge and orange rind spiral.

115 **Passion Fruit Margarita**

Serves 1

lime wedge and coarse sea salt, for rimming
1½ measures tequila gold
1 measure Cointreau
1 teaspoon passion fruit syrup
1 measure fresh lime juice
flesh and seeds of 1 passion fruit
ice cubes
lime wedges, to decorate

Moisten the rim of a margarita glass with a lime wedge and dip it in the salt. Put the tequila, Cointreau, passion fruit syrup, lime juice and half the passion fruit flesh and seeds in a cocktail shaker with some ice. Shake well then double-strain into a margarita glass. Add the remaining passion fruit flesh and decorate with lime wedges.

exciting & unusual

Pale Original

4 measures tequila gold
2 measures fresh lime juice
4 teaspoons ginger syrup
2 measures guava juice
crushed ice
grated lime rind, to decorate

Serves 2

Put the tequila, lime juice, ginger syrup and guava juice in a blender with some crushed ice and blend until slushy. Pour into hurricane glasses and decorate with grated lime rind.

exciting & unusual

117

Rude Cosmopolitan

Serves 8

300 ml (½ pint) tequila gold
200 ml (7 fl oz) Cointreau
200 ml (7 fl oz) cranberry juice
100 ml (3½ fl oz) fresh lime
    juice
ice cubes
8 orange rind spirals, to
    decorate

Mix the tequila, Cointreau, cranberry juice and fresh lime juice together in a large jug. Half-fill a cocktail shaker with ice. Pour in one-quarter of the mixture, shake well then strain into 2 chilled cocktail glasses. Repeat until the mixture is divided between 8 glasses. Decorate the drinks with a garnish of orange peel.

exciting & unusual

118

Mockingbird

Serves 2

2½ measures tequila
1½ measures green crème de
    menthe
2½ measures fresh lime juice
ice cubes
lemon rind spirals, to decorate

Pour the tequila, crème de
menthe and lime juice into a
cocktail shaker. Add some ice
cubes, shake vigorously for
about 10 seconds then strain
into 2 chilled cocktail glasses.
Decorate each with a lemon
rind spiral.

119

Avondale Habit

Serves 1

3 strawberries
dash sugar syrup (see page 9)
4 mint leaves
crushed ice
1½ measures brandy
freshly cracked black pepper
2 teaspoons crème de menthe
mint sprig and strawberry half,
    to decorate

Muddle the strawberries, sugar syrup and mint leaves together in an old-fashioned glass. Almost fill the glass with crushed ice, then add the brandy and cracked pepper. Stir and add more crushed ice then lace the drink with crème de menthe. Decorate with a mint sprig and strawberry half.

exciting & unusual

Spiced Sidecar

Serves 2

juice of 1 lemon
2 measures Morgan
    Spiced Rum
2 measures brandy
2 measures Cointreau
ice cubes
lemon and orange rind
    spirals, to decorate

Put the lemon juice, rum, brandy and Cointreau in a cocktail shaker with some ice cubes and shake well. Strain into 2 old-fashioned glasses filled with ice and decorate with lemon and orange spirals.

Big City Dog

Serves 2

4 dashes Peychaud's bitters
2 measures brandy
1 measure green
    Chartreuse
1 measure cherry brandy
ice cubes

Put 2 dashes bitters into each of 2 brandy balloons and swirl to coat the inside. Turn the glasses upside down and let drain. Put the brandy, green Chartreuse and cherry brandy in a mixing glass with some ice cubes and stir well, then double-strain into the brandy balloons.

exciting & unusual

122

Alexander Baby

Serves 2

ice cubes
4 measures dark rum
2 measures crème de cacao
1 measure double cream
grated nutmeg, to decorate

Put some ice cubes in a cocktail shaker and pour the rum, crème de cacao and cream over the ice. Shake until a frost forms, then strain into 2 chilled cocktail glasses. Sprinkle grated nutmeg on top and serve.

123

Pussyfoot

Serves 2

crushed ice
3 measures white rum
2 measures double cream
2 measures pineapple juice
2 measures fresh lime juice
2 measures cherry juice
pineapple slices and cocktail
cherries, to decorate

Put some crushed ice in a blender and add the rum, cream, pineapple juice, lime juice and cherry juice. Blend at high speed for 15–20 seconds, then pour into 2 hurricane glasses. Decorate each with a slice of pineapple and a cherry.

Vanilla Daisy

2 measures bourbon whiskey
1 measure fresh lemon juice
1 measure vanilla syrup
crushed ice
1 teaspoon grenadine
cocktail cherries, to decorate

Serves 1

Put the bourbon, lemon juice and vanilla syrup in a cocktail shaker with some crushed ice and shake well. Strain into an old-fashioned glass filled with crushed ice then drizzle the grenadine through the drink. Decorate with cocktail cherries.

exciting & unusual

125

Luigi

Serves 2

ice cubes
2 measures fresh orange juice
2 measures dry vermouth
1 measure Cointreau
2 measures grenadine
4 measures gin
blood orange slices, to
    decorate

Put some ice cubes in a mixing glass. Pour the orange juice, vermouth, Cointreau, grenadine and gin over the ice and stir vigorously. Strain into 2 chilled cocktail glasses, decorate each with an orange slice and serve.

126

Cowboy

Serves 4

4 measures chilled
    butterscotch schnapps
2 measure Bailey's Irish Cream

Pour a measure of schnapps
into each of 4 shot glasses,
then float the Bailey's on top
by pouring it over the back of
a spoon in contact with the
liquid surface.

Cowgirl

4 measures chilled peach
   schnapps
2 measures Bailey's Irish Cream
4 peach wedges

Serves 4

Pour a measure of chilled
schnapps into each of 4 shot
glasses, then layer the Bailey's on
top (see opposite). Place a peach
wedge on the rim of each glass,
to be eaten after the shot has
been drunk.

exciting & unusual

189

alcohol-free

Pink Melon Delight

Serves 2–3

150 g (5 oz) melon, cut
    into dice
150 g (5 oz) strawberries,
    plus extra to decorate
2–3 scoops orange sorbet
300 ml (½ pint) ginger ale

Put the melon, strawberries
and orange sorbet in a
blender and blend at high
speed for 15 seconds.
Gently stir in the ginger
ale, pour into wine glasses
and decorate each with
a strawberry.

Kiwi, Grape and Lime Crush

Serves 3–4

250 g (8 oz) kiwi fruit
300 ml (½ pint) white grape
    juice
juice of 2 limes
crushed ice, to serve
kiwi fruit slices, to decorate

Put the kiwi fruit, grape
juice and lime juice in a
food processor and process
until smooth. Serve in
glasses over crushed ice
and decorate with slices of
kiwi fruit.

alcohol-free

Right: Pink Melon Delight

130

Grapefruit Mint Cooler

Serves 6

125 g (4 oz) sugar
125 ml (4 fl oz) water
handful of mint sprigs
juice of 4 large lemons
450 ml (¾ pint) grapefruit juice
crushed ice
250 ml (8 fl oz) soda water
mint sprigs, to decorate

Put the sugar and water in a heavy-based saucepan and stir over a low heat until dissolved. Leave to cool. Crush the mint leaves and stir them into the syrup. Cover and leave to stand for about 12 hours, then strain into a jug. Add the lemon and grapefruit juices to the strained syrup and stir well. Fill 6 old-fashioned glasses or tumblers with crushed ice and pour the grapefruit into the glasses. Top up with the soda water and decorate with mint sprigs.

131

Cranberry Crush

Serves 15

crushed ice
1.8 litres (3 pints) cranberry
 juice
600 ml (1 pint) orange juice
600 ml (1 pint) ginger ale
orange and lemon wedges, to
 decorate

Half-fill a large punch bowl
with crushed ice. Pour in the
cranberry and orange juices
and stir to mix. Top up with the
ginger ale and decorate with
orange and lemon wedges.
Serve immediately.

alcohol-free

132

Prohibition Punch

Serves 25–30

125 ml (4 fl oz) sugar syrup (see page 9)
350 ml (12 fl oz) lemon juice
900 ml (1½ pints) apple juice
ice cubes
2.5 litres (4 pints) ginger ale
orange slices, to decorate

Stir together the sugar syrup, lemon and apple juices in a large chilled jug. Add the ice cubes and pour in the ginger ale. Decorate with orange slices and serve.

Apple and Strawberry Cup

500 g (1 lb) very ripe strawberries, hulled
2 tablespoons caster sugar
juice of 1 large orange
sparkling apple juice, to top up
ice cubes

Serves 6

Place the strawberries in a bowl and bruise them with a wooden spoon. Sprinkle with the sugar and orange juice, then cover and leave to stand for 1 hour. Pour the fruit cup into a jug, top it up with sparkling apple juice and ice cubes and serve.

alcohol-free

134

Limeade

Serves 8

6 limes
125 g (4 oz) caster sugar
750 ml (1¼ pints) boiling water
pinch of salt
ice cubes
lime wedges and mint leaves,
    to decorate

Halve the limes then squeeze the juice into a large jug. Put the squeezed lime halves into another heatproof jug with the sugar and boiling water and leave to infuse for 15 minutes. Add the salt, give the infusion a good stir, then strain it into the jug holding the lime juice. Add half a dozen ice cubes, cover and chill for 2 hours. To serve, place 3–4 ice cubes in each glass and pour the limeade over. Add a lime wedge and a mint leaf to decorate.

alcohol-free

135

Pink Tonic

Serves 1

2–3 dashes Angostura bitters
4–6 ice cubes
250 ml (8 fl oz) tonic water
lime wedge, to decorate

Drop the bitters over ice in a
tumbler, add the tonic water
and stir well. Decorate with a
lime wedge.

alcohol-free

136

Shirley Temple

Serves 4

ice cubes
4 dashes grenadine
ginger ale, to top up
cocktail cherries, to
    decorate

Put 4–5 ice cubes in each
of 4 glasses. Add a dash of
grenadine and top up with
the ginger ale. Decorate
each glass with 2 cherries
on a cocktail stick.

137

Honeymoon

Serves 1

crushed ice
1 measure maple syrup or
    clear honey
4 teaspoons fresh lime juice
1 measure orange juice
1 measure apple juice
cocktail cherry, to decorate

Put some crushed ice in a
cocktail shaker and add
the maple syrup or honey,
lime juice, orange juice
and apple juice. Shake
well then strain into a
chilled cocktail glass.
Decorate with a cherry on
a cocktail stick.

alcohol-free

Right: Shirley Temple

138 Iced Apple Tea

Serves 6–8

¾ pint chilled weak tea
450 ml (¾ pint) apple juice
juice of 1 lemon
1 teaspoon sugar (optional)
ice cubes
orange and lemon slices and
    mint sprigs, to decorate

Mix the tea with the apple juice, lemon juice and sugar, if using. Add plenty of ice and decorate with the lemon and orange slices and mint sprigs. Serve in tumblers or tea glasses.

alcohol-free

206

Iced Mint Tea

Serves 4

12 mint sprigs
1 lemon, finely chopped
1 tablespoon sugar
1.2 litres (2 pints) weak tea,
    strained
ice cubes
lemon slices, to decorate

Chop 4 of the mint sprigs and put them in a large heatproof jug with the lemon and sugar. Pour the tea into the jug and set aside to infuse for 20–30 minutes. Strain into another jug and chill until required. To serve, pour into tumblers or tall glasses filled with ice and decorate each glass with slices of lemon and some of the remaining mint sprigs.

Florentine Coffee

Serves 2

espresso coffee
2 drops almond essence
2 sugar cubes (optional)

Pour the coffee into 2 warmed cups or heatproof glasses. Add a drop of almond essence and a sugar cube, if using, to each cup or glass and stir.

alcohol-free

Romanov Fizz

Serves 2

8–10 ripe strawberries, hulled
125 ml (4 fl oz) orange juice
2 ice cubes
125 ml (4 fl oz) soda water

Put the strawberries and orange juice in a food processor and process until smooth. Place 1 ice cube in each of 2 sour glasses or wine glasses and add the strawberry liquid. Pour the soda water into the food processor, process very briefly and use to top up the glasses. Stir briskly and serve.

Dandy

Serves 2

6 measures apple juice
2 measures strawberry syrup
2 measures lime juice
20 blackberries
cracked ice
blackberries and mint sprigs, to decorate

Put the apple juice, strawberry syrup, lime juice and the blackberries in a food processor with some cracked ice and process until smooth. Pour into 2 tall glasses. Decorate each with a blackberry and a mint sprig.

Right: Dandy

143

Carrot Cream

Serves 4

250 ml (8 fl oz) carrot juice
300 ml (½ pint) single cream
4 egg yolks
125 ml (4 fl oz) fresh orange
   juice
20 ice cubes
slices of orange, to decorate

Put the carrot juice, cream, egg yolks and orange juice into a cocktail shaker and shake well. Divide the ice cubes among 4 tall glasses and pour the carrot drink on top. Decorate with orange slices and serve immediately. Serve with straws.

alcohol-free

hair of the dog

144

Corpse Reviver

Serves 1

3 cracked ice cubes
2 measures brandy
1 measure calvados
1 measure sweet vermouth
apple slice, to decorate

Put the ice, brandy, calvados
and sweet vermouth in a
cocktail shaker and shake
until a frost forms. Strain into
a tumbler and decorate with
an apple slice.

hair of the dog

145

Knockout

Serves 1

4–5 ice cubes
1 measure dry vermouth
½ measure white crème de
  menthe
2 measures gin
drop Pernod
lemon slice, to serve

Put the ice cubes in a
mixing glass. Pour the
vermouth, crème de
menthe and gin over the
ice, stir vigorously, then
strain into a chilled old-
fashioned glass. Add the
Pernod and serve with a
lemon slice.

146

Prairie Oyster

Serves 1

2 measures brandy
1 egg yolk
1 teaspoon wine vinegar
dash Tabasco sauce
dash Worcestershire sauce
pinch of cayenne pepper

Put the brandy, egg yolk,
vinegar, Tabasco and
Worcestershire sauces and
cayenne in a wine glass.
Stir gently without breaking
the egg yolk.

Bullshot

6 ice cubes (optional)
1½ measures vodka
4 measures beef consommé
    (hot or chilled)
dash Worcestershire sauce
salt and pepper

Serves 1

Put the ice cubes, if using, in a
cocktail shaker and add the
vodka, consommé and
Worcestershire sauce and season
lightly with salt and pepper. Shake
well. Strain into a large glass or
a handled heatproof glass, if
serving hot.

Variation
As a variation, try 1 measure
vodka, 1 measure tomato juice
and 1 measure beef consommé.
Mix the ingredients in a tall glass
half-filled with ice. Add a squeeze
of lemon.

hair of the dog

148

Bloody Maria

Serves 1

1 lime wedge, celery salt and
    black pepper, for rimming
1¼ measures tequila
2 teaspoons medium sherry
2 dashes Tabasco sauce
4 dashes Worcestershire sauce
1 tablespoon fresh lime juice
100 ml (3½ fl oz) fresh
    tomato juice
cayenne pepper
4–5 ice cubes
celery stick, lime wedge and
    basil sprig, to decorate

Dampen the rim of a glass with
a lime wedge then dip into
celery salt and black pepper.
Shake the rest of the
ingredients vigorously in a
cocktail shaker, then pour into
the rimmed glass. Decorate
with the celery stick, lime
wedge and a basil sprig.

149

Virgin Mary

Serves 1

4 measures tomato juice
ice cubes
½ measure lemon juice
2 dashes Worcestershire
    sauce
1 dash Tabasco sauce
celery stick, to decorate

Pour the tomato juice into
a glass over ice cubes, add
the lemon juice and
Worcestershire and
Tabasco sauces and stir
well. Decorate with a
celery stick and serve.

150

Kamikaze

Serves 1

6 cracked ice cubes
½ measure vodka
½ measure Curaçao
½ measure fresh lime juice

Put the cracked ice in a
cocktail shaker and add
the vodka, Curaçao and
lime juice. Shake until a
frost forms, then strain into
a shot glass.

Right: Kamikaze

hair of the dog

Acknowledgements

Octopus Publishing Group Ltd/Jean Cazals 37, 79
centre right, 93 /Stephen Conroy 2-3, 5 centre right
top, 10-11, 12-13, 17, 27, 71, 81, 87, 105, 113, 115,
137, 167 bottom right, 177, 213 top right, 215
/Sandra Lane 5 top right, 147 centre right, 155, 161,
197, 213 bottom right, 221 /Neil Mersh 5 centre left
top, 15, 21, 40-41, 41 centre right, 47, 49, 53, 65, 67,
78-79, 91, 101, 108-109, 111, 121, 131, 133, 143, 190-
191, 195, 211 /Peter Myers 13 bottom right, 29
/Juliet Piddington 79 top right, 95 /William Reavell
1, 3 right, 5 top left, 5 bottom right, 5 bottom left, 5
centre right bottom, 5 centre left bottom, 6-7, 8-9,
13 top right, 13 centre right, 23, 25, 31, 35, 38, 39, 41
top right, 41 bottom right, 43, 55, 59, 63, 73, 79
bottom right, 83, 85,99,107, 109 top right, 109
centre right, 109 bottom right, 117, 123, 125, 129,
135, 139, 141, 146-147, 147 top right, 147 bottom
right, 151, 157, 159, 165, 166-167, 167 top right, 167
centre right, 169, 173, 179, 183, 187, 191 top right,
191 centre right, 191 bottom right, 193, 201, 203,
205, 209, 212-213 left, 213 centre right, 21

commissioning editor
Sarah Ford

editor
Jo Lethaby

editorial assistant
Kristy Richardson

executive art editor
Peter Burt

production manager
Louise Hall

picture research
Jennifer Veall